THE CRICHTON

AN ANNIVERSARY RE-IMAGINING

An Anthology of New Writing

from

Crichton Writers

In Commemoration of The Bicentenary of

The Founding Bequest of

The Crichton Royal Institution

and

In Celebration of

The Twentieth Anniversary of

The Crichton Writers Group

Published by Crichton Writers 2024

in association with Coronach Press

ISBN 978-1-8382997-0-5

www.crictonwriters.wordpress.com

© images — as credited in end notes
with particular thanks to NHS Dumfries and Galloway
Crichton Royal Hospital Collection, held by the Heritage
Service, Dumfries and Galloway Council

Cover: *Crichton Royal Institution from the North-East*
(detail) anonymous artist, Crichton Royal Hospital
Collection

Editing & Design by Robin Leiper

Typeset in Franklin Gothic Book

Printed and bound by Bookvault

CONTENTS

THE PRESENT: AN ANIVERSARY REFLECTION

IN THE BEGINNING
A HISTORY RE-IMAGINED

In the Beginning — 1

Elizabeth Crichton – Letter   3rd August 1823

My dear Miriam,

It was so kind of you to write. I felt so guilty that you had to learn of James' death from my cousin Louisa. All I can say is that the period after James died passed in a whirl. I scarcely noticed the time and must confess to shedding many tears when alone. Moreover, I am guilty of neglecting to write to you for many months before that. There seemed so little to tell you as life went on in its uneventful accustomed way. I can tell that you received little detail from Louisa, so I will recount all that happened in those weeks. I can also impart to you, my dearest friend, my innermost thoughts.

Here I am, alone except for the servants. I feel as if a giant whirlwind has swept away life as we – I – knew it. James' death was such a surprise. He wasn't a young man, of course, but one day he was out and about as usual, seeing friends for coffee or conducting business, and the next he was in bed. He was feverish and struggling for breath. The day after, Dr McTurk wanted him to be taken to hospital, but he refused to go. Janet, the nurse, and I bathed him constantly with cool water from the icehouse, but to no effect.

Three days later the doctor returned and pronounced him dead. In his wake came our old friend, the Reverend Henry Duncan of Ruthwell Parish, to pray over James, and arrange a meeting with me and Alistair, James' eldest brother, to discuss funeral arrangements. You may recall that James had first known Henry when he invested in the Trustee Savings Bank which Henry started up in 1810, the year we married. Janet offered to lay James out herself but I wanted to help her. It was not the first time that I have assisted at such a thing. Those few hours of quiet brought some peace.

A day later Henry returned. Alistair arrived soon after and the three of us set to our task. Firstly, we decided on the readings and hymns – I was able to call to mind some of James' favourites. Next, and rather more contentious, the readers of the Gospel and the Eulogy must be determined. I wished to speak of my husband but was told it was not seemly. Therefore, I insisted that I, with a few additions from Alistair, should compose the Eulogy, which was reluctantly agreed by my companions.

There was no time to gather my wits that day. Downstairs the rest of James' siblings, with some of the younger children, had gathered to view him, offer their condolences, and partake of a collation of cold cuts, washed down with plenty of small beer, or, for the children, cool spring water. Watching the children, I felt a stabbing in my heart, which once upon a time was a constant from about a year after we married until I knew that I was past the age to conceive. James never reproached me for the lack of an heir, but that unspoken longing and mourning for what never came burdened my heart for many a year, although I tried to remain bright and cheerful when in James' company.

The funeral, held in the familiar old Ruthwell Church, beside the Ruthwell Cross which commemorates our ancient Christian faith, was everything I and James' family could have wanted. It was dignified and prayerful, yet Henry managed to interject some of his own light-hearted memories of my husband, which reminded all present of James' sense of humour. Alistair read my Eulogy with fitting solemnity, giving James due credit for his business acumen and his commitment to me, his siblings and my family members.

We returned to the house for the funeral spread, in which my excellent Cook, Martha, had outdone herself. Everyone had their fill, and still there were enough leftovers to feed the household the next day. Alistair and his wife, Sarah, stayed the night, so that I might not be alone on this, the first night when I truly felt my new status as a widow. Their children were taken to James' third brother's house. Robert has always been a firm favourite with all the children in James' family and in mine.

A week later, at two o'clock on the dot, Mr Dobie, the family solicitor, arrived, with a large black case. He was followed by a servant bearing an armful of documents in manila folders. For some unknown reason these filled me with apprehension. Alistair ushered them in to the dining room, the only place with a table large enough to accommodate all the paperwork. James' other siblings arrived at half past two and settled themselves round our rarely used mahogany table. Henry was also present, by my personal invitation.

Pince-nez secured on his nose, Mr Dobie began the solemn reading of the Will. As I already knew, James had left the bulk of his wealth to me, with a generous bequest for each of his siblings. There was no grumbling, but rather an appreciative murmuring of satisfaction on all sides. However, the large pile of folders remained untouched. Despite the sadness of the occasion, we were all agog with curiosity. Mr Dobie moved the Will to one side and gestured to his servant to move the files within reach of all. It transpired that these documents related to James' many and various investments.

Mr Dobie began thus: "I do not intend at this point to read the full details of these documents before us. Suffice to say, that Dr James Crichton was a wise and prudent investor. He investigated every potential source of income and only acquired those which were properly audited by lawyers skilled in financial transactions The total worth of his investments and other income, after allowing for the personal bequests which we have just heard, is £100,000, to be used by Mrs Elizabeth Crichton for charitable purposes. In this endeavour she will be aided by myself, Dr Henry Duncan, and James' eldest brother, Alistair, together with any Trustees that we see fit to appoint."

There was total silence for at least two minutes, during which I could scarcely breathe. I was daunted by the vast amount of money entrusted to me, but I knew that the men appointed would help me set about my task. I was also touched by James' faith in me. If he had believed in me, I felt I must be capable of undertaking this enterprise.

I have been much occupied in deciding what I should do with this bequest. I keep returning to an idea which James and I had often discussed in recent years, the provision of a local University here in Dumfries. This would enable young men in the area to select their study material from a wide choice of disciplines, and thus enhance their opportunities for a better life for them and their families. The town of Dumfries would greatly benefit from such a project. I still need to discuss this with Henry and Alistair, who will give me their opinions on my idea and discover how we may advance it.

In the meantime, my dear Miriam, I would like it very much if you could see your way to visiting me here. I should much enjoy your company, if only for a few days.

I remain your loving friend,

Elizabeth xxx

Linda Powell

In the Beginning — 2

Elizabeth Crichton – Diary Extract   May 1834

For ten years James and I strove, with the assistance of our dear friend the Reverend Henry Duncan, Minister of Ruthwell Parish Church, who started the first Trustee Savings Bank the year James and I were married, to realize our great wish to found a seat of learning in Dumfries. Henry was such a good friend to James, and he has been a tower of strength to me, during the 10 years since James' death, in my efforts to establish a College of University status in Dumfries for the education of poor scholars.

Sadly, our efforts have been blocked by the four Scottish Universities, who guard their positions jealously, and a recent change of Government has resulted in an administration less sympathetic to our cause. It has been decided that the scheme cannot go ahead without government financial support in spite of the £85,000 set aside for the project. Also, my brother-in-law has made things more difficult by contesting

James' Will through the courts of law, a fight in which I have, at last, been successful, but it has been costly!

I think it is now time to give up on our dream. The Trustees and I have decided to endow a lunatic asylum on the edge of Dumfries and so, we have procured a suitable piece of land with magnificent views over Criffel and the River. The land amounts to 40 acres of the Mountainhall Estate at Hillhead. I am determined that my hospital will be the best in Europe, not only in the treatment of patients, but also in its architecture and surroundings, which will be so important to the wellbeing of the inmates. To this end, I have employed the architect, William Burn, to design the hospital. I have seen his plans for Inverness Castle, which is nearly completed and which will be a really splendid building in the fashionable Scottish baronial style I like so much. It is just what I have in mind for the Crichton Hospital; a spacious building, built in local red sandstone, resembling the palace of a peer, airy, elevated and elegant and surrounded by extensive grounds and gardens, for the benefit and enjoyment of the patients.

Beverley Vaux

Crichton Royal Institution.

The Phrenologist and the Widow

Elizabeth sat down in a chair indicated by the man with receding hairline, muttonchop sideburns, high wing collar and maroon velvet jacket. He shook her hand then settled himself back down into his own chair, behind a large mahogany desk.

"Mrs Crichton?" She smiled.

"You have come such a long way. I trust your carriage was comfortable, at least. May I offer you some refreshment? Some tea?"

"Thank you, but no."

"A glass of water, then?"

"You are very kind, sir, but really, we stopped several times on the way here, thank you. However, I have pressing business with you and I will not be able to rest until I have discussed it."

"I wonder what can be so pressing to bring you here in this dreadful weather."

Elizabeth sat, hands in her lap, took a deep breath and began. "You may or may not be aware that my husband left me some property and a sizeable amount of money to spend on whatever project I choose, provided it is approved by the trustees."

Dr Browne said nothing, so she continued. "Initially I wanted to create a university, but Edinburgh universities have blocked that aspiration. However, this may turn out to be a blessing in disguise. I want to create an institute for lunatics, a progressive one, the best of its kind. And I believe you can help me with this."

He raised his eyebrows but still said nothing. Instead, he picked up and shuffled the small pile of papers he had been looking at before Elizabeth's entry and put them into his desk drawer.

Elizabeth pressed on. "I want to appoint you to become Crichton's first medical superintendent, and to implement your ideas of both occupational therapy and art therapy. I read your book *What Asylums Were, Are, and Ought To Be* and find your ideas on the moral treatment of lunatics most exciting; an innovative approach to the care of mental patients. I may not have a medical background, but I want to be involved, to be in regular discussion with you about patients' progress."

Dr Browne eyed her for a few seconds then said, "For the last one hundred years or so the insane have been treated as wild animals, not held responsible for their actions and kept locked up in appalling conditions, enduring treatments like bloodletting, irritant chemicals, being whipped, beaten, and starved. How do you think they should be treated?"

"From what I've heard and read about you I understand your approach is one of moral management, based on humane psychosocial care of the patient."

He nodded. "My work here in Montrose Asylum has shown that social groupings are important, and shifting symptom patterns are often reflected in patients' dreams."

"And you use art mediums too, to provide insights into patients' conditions?"

"Yes. If we can enable patients to express themselves artistically the works not only provide us with insights into patients' conditions, they're also an important part of their treatment and recovery. Writing, painting, music – these forms encourage creative expression and operate by providing a person with a safe space to express their emotions, allowing them to feel more in control over their life. For example, Art therapy can help people improve cognitive and sensory motor function, self-esteem, self-awareness, and emotional resilience. It may also aid in resolving conflicts and reducing distress."

"Oh, Dr Browne, this is so exciting! I'm prepared to offer you a position with a salary of £350 per annum and will build you a separate house for you and your family within the grounds. My architect, William Burn, has designed the buildings and construction began three years ago. He assures me that the hospital will be completed and opened as the Crichton Institution for Lunatics next year. With you at the helm as Medical Superintendent I am sure that we shall be an outstanding medical facility for the treatment of the insane. Will you join us??

Kriss Nichol

Dr Flora Murray

I withdrew money from the bank today. The lass who waved me over the grey carpeting to her desk danced her fingers over the keyboard.

'How would you like the cash?

'I'd like a one-hundred-pound note, please.'
Her fingers paused and she leaned back in her chair to look at me.

'Aah,' she said, and raised quizzical eyebrows to an assistant beside her. 'We don't hold that denomination at the front counter,' her colleague confirmed. She nodded me over to a window where a supervisor was sorting through notes. 'It's okay, I'll get you one.' My dancing fingers friend rose from her seat.

'Thank you, but before you do, can you tell me if it displays an image of Dr Flora Murray? I'd like to have the note because I believe that she's featured on it.'

'I've no idea.' She looked towards her colleague again. In unison they said, 'Who is Dr Flora Murray?'

'Dr Murray qualified as a doctor, one of the first women to do so, at the beginning of the 20th century. She became a medical pioneer and a prime mover in promoting the rights of women. Her birth place was Dalton, near Dumfries.'

'I thought that there must be a local connection, I'll see if I can find out.'

The assistant nipped across and conferred with the note-sorting lady who promptly disappeared into a room at the back.

Dr Flora had caught my interest when I learned that during her medical training she had worked as a medical assistant at Crichton Royal Hospital. The Crichton ran a progressive, holistic operation. Her work there taught her the importance of treating minds as well as wounds, an invaluable asset when she later set up a field hospital in France to treat men wounded in the First World War. In 1916 the government invited her to set up a Military Hospital in London to continue this work. She was a humanitarian, passionate about women's rights, and she treated suffragettes on hunger strike. Dr Flora was awarded a CBE three years after the war ended.

The lady emerged from the depths of the bank waving a note.
'It is her!' she beamed.

My assistant studied the note as she brought it over, holding it out for me to see. Exquisite shades of green and gold brought in mind aquamarine seas and gleaming sands but the most prominent feature was a striking image of Dr Flora, presumably taken from a portrait. I looked into her steady gaze holding knowledge, wisdom and compassion, saw her fine, straight nose, her firm mouth and the script underneath declaring Dr Flora Murray, Scottish Medical Pioneer.

'My supervisor says that it's the first polymer

Bank of Scotland note to celebrate the contribution of a significant Scottish person.'

'That's all very well and I can see why they put her on a £100 note as it's a century this year since her death, but I do wonder how many of us draw notes of such a high value. It's not exactly going to tell her story to the masses.'

'Mmm...do you see the wee ambulance etched on it and the stretcher bearers are ladies!'

'I do and here's a medical instrument, and in this tiny drawing she's sitting at her desk.

We were absorbed by the details and agreed that best of all was the transparent window hosting a holographic foil image of the Dr Flora portrait. On the obverse side, the holograph shone just as brightly alongside a picture of Sir Walter Scott, novelist and poet.

My helper moved to her station and once again her fingers flew over the keys. She looked up as I began to pop my bank card into the machine.

'Aaah, do you have a Bank of Scotland card? Or a Lloyds Bank card?'

I had neither.

'Then I'm afraid that I can't do this transaction,' her voice tailed off.

Her colleague saw me stare at the Dr Flora note, just out of reach. 'Pop across to the cash machine there, withdraw £100 and we'll do a swap.'

It was a thrill to have the crisp banknote in my hand at last. It had not been easy to come by and I thought that possibly only a very few of us can say that we have held one which celebrates Dr Flora Murray's colossal contribution to medicine in the early twentieth century.

Christine Ashworth

THE CAMPUS PAST & PRESENT
MEMORIES & RESPONSES

The Horticultural Show

The people of Dumfries were invited by flyer to attend The Horticultural Show at Crichton Royal Institution and it must have been a fascinating day out for them. This was sometime in the late 1800's.

It seems, however, that the weather forecast was not at all kind. These days, the show would most likely have been cancelled due to health and safety concerns. Not so this one!

By patronage of St Swithin, the show must go on!

'The rain it reigneth every day!'

Excerpts from the programme as follows:

1. Gardeners' Competition. Competitors and judges to be on the ground with the First Dew, and to enjoy the grounds and rain until 11.am.

2.The inmates to inspect Greenhouses, Waterworks, Dew-points and other hydropathic arrangements from 11 to 2.

3.The Gates and Waterspouts to be opened to the public at 12.

4.The pensive and pluvious public to dispose and disport themselves like "dolphins in a tropic sea" amid "dew-sprinkled bowers", upon such part of terra firma as may remain.

5.The public to be admitted to an aquatic entertainment in the North Flower Garden, where singing, dancing, gymnastics (not diving or swimming) will be provided under the auspices of the Crichton Chorus Singers, Carlisle Band and the Messrs

Hutchinson, from 3 to 4. The songs to be of this following class: "The meeting of the Waters", "I'm afloat", "Tell her I love her while the clouds drop rain" and "Tak your auld cloke about ye".

6. The Bowling Green has been shaved and will be washed should the public desire to conclude the Fete by a Dance thereon, or a Teetotal Promenade. N.B. Shower baths and douches to be had within, Dissolving views of the Nith upon a grand scale. Sky fountains without the House at all hours during the Fete. Ladies to be provided with pattens and parapluies.

What a wonderfully humorous document! I can imagine all the ladies in their most waterproof skirts dancing on the bowling green as they splashed through the puddles, and the gardening competitors huddled in small groups, rain dripping from their hats, for it is only the ladies who are provided with parapluies!

In case you wondered if those song titles were real, here are the words to one of them.

Tell her I love her while the clouds drop rain by William Shield.

> TELL her I love her while the clouds drop rain,
> Or while there's water in the pathly main;
> Tell her I love her till this life be o'er,
> And then my ghost shall visit this sweet shore:
> Tell her I only ask she'll think on me—
> I'll love her while there's salt within the sea:
> Tell her all this; tell it, tell it o'er and o'er,
> I'll love her while there's salt within the sea:
> Tell her all this; tell it o'er and o'er;
> The anchor's weigh'd, or I would tell her more.

I'm Afloat was first published in 1841, written by Eliza Cook, and is a hymn in praise of piracy.

Tak your Auld Cloke About Ye, also called *Queen Mary's Lamentation*, was written in 1823. Here is the final verse:

> Bell, my wife, she lo'es nae strife
> ☐But she will guide me if she can;
> And, to maintain an easy life,
> ☐I aft maun yield, though I'm gudeman.
> Noughts to be won at woman's hand,
> ☐Unless ye gi'e her a' the plea;
> Then I'll leave aff where I began,
> ☐And tak' my auld cloke about me.

Carol Price

The Crichton Doll's House

I worked in the Doll's House for four years. It was a modern, rectangular box, with a kitchen, a wood workshop, a stimulus-free room, two small playrooms and a tiny office, the latter used by the Child Psychiatry Department's two occupational therapists. The office suited us well: we didn't spend much time in it. I was fresh out of college, but Sheila had raised two sons.

We reckoned that we had the best jobs in the Child Psychiatry Team. Teachers had to persuade children – whose educational experience had often been totally negative – that yes, they wanted to learn! They really did! And they could, with a little help.... Nurses at the three houses: Ladyfield West, Ladyfield East and Hannahfield, had to comfort homesick kiddies at bedtime, break up fights, console those whose parents didn't turn up when expected, and cope with angry, unpredictable outbursts. Psychologists had to administer complicated tests. Social Workers drove the length and breadth of southern Scotland, to the Central Belt and occasionally beyond, unfankling family complexities and supporting parents who, themselves, had often lacked good parenting. For us, children turned up on the dot and banged on the door, eager for their session.

On the day of my interview (in August 1976), when the Head O.T. took me through the locked gate into Ladyfield West's playground, a skinny red-headed lad ran up and took my hand.

'Are you my new O.T.?'

'I hope so,' I replied.

'Hooray!' he shouted and dashed off to spread the good news.

Boys left the workshop in a stour of sawdust, brandishing guns and swords: blunt swords, very blunt swords, I hasten to add. Sticky-fingered girls and boys left the kitchen clutching their own warm bakes: chocolate buns, jam tarts, gingerbread men, sponges oozing red jam and fairy cakes, lavishly iced.

For imaginative play we offered a dressing up box, puppets, and dolls. We provided paper and paints. Our super-popular dartboard didn't have numbers on it. Instead, you targeted pictures: men, women and children, authority figures or pets. It could be quite revealing.

At team meetings we had serious discussions about assessment and treatment, developmental levels, coordination and cooperation, self-esteem, and self-control, but for the kids, the Doll's House was where you played, enjoyed treats and let off steam.

Everyone loved the Doll's House – except, of course, the cleaning ladies.

Barbara Mearns

Round and Round the Cairncross Room

Whee! I run my hand around the table
I watch that look. I love it!
The faster I birl, the more shoulders shiver
The grandfather in the corner observes
And stops, to enjoy the fun
The time is twelve noon

I pass this way often, unseen
The frisson of surprise at the slight draught
Always excites me
I see anxious faces as they listen to
the history of the Cairncross
Surgeons who operated here
Students in the gallery above
And I sense a lack of attention

Some look as if they've seen a ghost, so
I do a final whirl which has them
Reaching for their bags and brollies
They look at the clock, check their watches
The timepiece in the corner stands
Silent, at midday

The last to leave swears he hears
Laughter
And then the gentle whoosh
As the pendulum begins once more.

Jane Richarson

The Ghost Child

As Kara laboured up the tight spiralling stone staircase, breath curling away above, her footfalls echoed loudly, seeming to come from all around. She consciously planted each foot firmly on the smooth-worn surfaces, lest she slip. These stairs seemed cold in more ways than one. A slip could mean broken bones, if not a broken neck. No one but her ever seemed to come up here risking their life. Cheap labour was done by cheap lives, it was always the way. She cleaned surfaces of dust that nobody would ever see. She shone the railings, the wood and marble surfaces that nobody but her remembered actually existed.

Kara was only dimly aware of the history of the grand old building that she cleaned but it was impossible to be unaware of the beauty: turrets with hidden garrets, bridges, balconies, acres of carved wooden furniture. She had heard that it had once been a lunatic asylum. Today it was a relic, the type of folly no-one built anymore, and no-one knew what to do with. This room at the top of the stairs was a good example: part of a high tower on the edge of a building containing hundreds of rooms, most of them hardly used these days. The current occupier was a university. A few students sat in small groups in some of the rooms, providing little animation to dispel the atmosphere of church like gloom that pervaded the building.

Placing her bucket down on a table and pulling her long black puffa jacket tighter around her Klara shivered as she picked up her cloth and ran it along the railings in the centre of the room where a huge hole in the floor looked down into the room below. That room had once been an operating theatre. She shuddered to imagine what kind of operations had been done in a Victorian mental asylum, trying not to think what was ingrained in these ancient surfaces. Currently the lower room was a library filled with bookshelves stacked with dusty books. In the middle of the room stood a massive round table. Kara enjoyed romantic daydreams, imagining herself as Queen Guinevere in an emerald green gown, sitting at the table with handsome King Arthur in silver armour by her side. It was a nice daydream in the summer. Just now she felt like Jadis, the white witch queen of Narnia.

The balcony saw little use these days. There were no performances taking place on the round table for spectators from above. Currently it was a storage space for around twenty large paintings propped against the walls. Above were round windows, like portholes into the pitch black void outside. The sky was cloudy and pregnant with the threat of snow. Not even a sliver of moon showed through the dense cloud to illuminate the scene.

A movement in the room below snagged the corner of her eye, making Kara jump with fright. She was only secure in this cavernous building knowing she was the only living thing larger than a spider. It was half past seven in the morning. There shouldn't be anyone else here for another hour when the first of the secretarial and teaching staff would start to arrive. Her mind leapt straight to murderous burglars. A cold sweat slicked her skin and her heart hammered in her chest. Kara wanted to shut out the horror but forced herself to look down.

What she saw puzzled and relieved her at the same time. She let out an involuntary gasp of relief. It was a child. A young blonde haired girl was skipping around the table below. The sound of humming filtered up in an unfamiliar tune. The girl's clothing was also unusual — a white dress, with an apron and a flared skirt that reached well below her knee, the dress decorated with ruffles and a high neck line. She wore black elaborately laced up boots and around her head a white silk ribbon, tied in a bow. Her hair was shoulder length and bounced with each skipping step. She seemed happy, slim but not under-nourished. She bounded around the room and out of Kara's view. Seconds later she reappeared, circling the table.

"Hello," Kara called.

It was the girl's turn to gasp in fright. She skidded to a halt, looking for the source of the voice. Seeing Kara, the girl visibly paled, like she'd been caught somewhere she was forbidden. Turning, the girl started to run towards the far corner of the room. This struck Kara as odd as the doorway from the library was on the opposite wall.

"It's ok, I'm not angry, what are you doing here?" Kara called out.

She was ignored. Kara turned and took the stone stairs two at a time, risking her neck recklessly. She ran into the library to see the girl was still running towards the far corner of the room — strange, as the girl had had more than enough time to reach the far wall before Kara got to the doorway. The girl appeared to have waited where Kara had last seen her until she was in view again.

The girl was running toward one of the library's antiquities, a grandfather clock, six foot high in dark mahogany. Kara trotted across the room towards her. As she did so, the girl reached for the right hand front of the clock where there was a heavy brass key which she turned, looking frantically back at Kara looming towards her. Opening the door which formed almost the entire front of the clock, the girl turned sideways and began sliding herself inside. Kara reached out a hand and touched the girl on her shoulder. As she did so something happened that she would never forget. A jolt of sensory chaos ran through her: she smelt the scent of the sun, tasted failure and knew what it was to touch the void at the end of the universe; her head filled with the roar of a breaking heart. As if by a hurricane blast, she was hurled upwards to land heavily, flat on her back in the middle of the round table.

Kara lay there groaning trying to recover her senses from the terrifying jumble of emotional energy that had rampaged through her. She managed to prop herself up on her elbows and look at the clock. Nothing was moving, the room was silent and still. Sitting up and rubbing her complaining back, she jumped down painfully and limped over to the clock.

"It's ok. I'm going to open the door. I just want to talk," said Kara.

She managed to sound braver than she felt. She tried the door and found it locked. The girl must have somehow turned the key from inside. Kara turned the key back and opened it. Empty. The girl was gone. Indeed the space inside the clock looked too small for her to have fitted into it.

Wondering if she had been knocked unconscious and lain there for longer than she imagined, Klara looked at her watch and saw the time was much as she'd expected. There was no way to tell if she'd been unconscious even for a few minutes. It was just possible that someone had come and unlocked the door and taken the girl away before she'd recovered consciousness.

Kara didn't believe in the supernatural, yet... She was finding it hard to believe that something explainable had happened here. There was a strong need to distance herself, get outside in the fresh air, at least out of this library. She turned and walked out, along the quiet corridors and through the foyer, past pictures she'd seen a hundred times before. Suddenly, in one of these she saw the girl she'd seen in the library. The same girl, wearing the same clothes as when she'd glimpsed her minutes before. She stood there, one of a class of schoolchildren from 1870. There was a list of names. The girl was identified as Elizabeth Huntley.

Chills ran up Kara's spine as she walked out of the building. But she would be back.

Scott Thow

The Pool

Look at me now, all glitter and bling, with a sparkling mosaic surround! Large new windows permit fresh light to flood in, illuminating the modern decor. Hospital workers enjoy a swim and a chat at lunchtime, share jokes, talk of NHS strikes and hoped-for improvements to their pay. When families come, their children scamper and splash in my scintillating tropical warmth, while the elderly and infirm delight in my healing embrace.

When I was built in 1938, as part of the Easterbrook therapeutic and recreation building, I had a more serious purpose: a "lunatics' hydrotherapy pool". Behind me there was a hairdressing salon, squash courts and an exercise room. I was plain then, with white tiles and small sub-basement windows to hide me from view. The water was not quite so warm but its hugging and caressing protection wrought its magic on bruised minds and broken bodies. Most patients left this place feeling cleansed, healed, and renewed. I hope all those who come here can feel the benefits of immersion in that most precious of elements—water!

Beverley Vaux

The Crichton Crypt V2. (23/11/23)

Abandoned archaic trolley, stands alone.
Chipped, cream-painted, metal frame
stark against the sandstone wall.
Arches block light, shadows fall.
Crypt, cold, empty, serene.
Trolley says what it means;
does not move an inch.
Evocative of a moment in time
wheels rattled on stone floors
carrying unfortunates
through tunnels
from the lunatic asylum.
Tortured souls weakened by madness
wheeled here to rest in peace
until the humanity of committal.

Christine Cameron

Spirits Abound

There is a tranquillity about the Crichton Grounds, as if the souls of those, long gone, are still there – walking with us and seeing what we see.

Some were the poorer residents of the Crichton Hall, whose existence was a fight to survive. Others, the better off, enjoyed a more luxurious setting. We can only imagine their lives and hope never to experience the plight of either group.

We know, of course, that Crichton Hall was built from the legacy that Dr James Crichton left for charitable purposes and was used to house the mentally ill. His wife Elizabeth was unaware of how the amazing venture she had undertaken would develop over the long decades after she founded it and might never have imagined that her initial hopes for a university on the site would eventually come to pass in the Millenium.

The statue of Elizabeth, which sits eloquently on the grounds, is a symbol of how highly she was and still is regarded.

The only way to capture the atmosphere of the campus is to spend time quietly wandering within it and breathing in the air around you. Even today, this place holds an unexplained magic, which will always be there, along with the spirits who guard it.

beautiful sandstone

a vision of peacefulness

capturing the mind

Eleanor Chesters

The Crichton Rock Garden

September still warm with a tinge
of bronze tipped leaf, bird song loud and clear
branches in gentle motion prompt the
the annual flutter of farewell
the sun, with latent heat, lingers on arboretum
to create shadow and secret corner
this, the Rock Garden
a place of peace, regrowth, regeneration

an insistent repetitive sound interrupts
rat-a-tat-tat! rat-a-tat-tat!
not a woodpecker? No
for voice now accompanies the cacophony
Tranquillity, as I happen upon the eponymous tree,
is no more

I came in search of the past
now catapulted into the present
calm thought has ceased
the source as yet unseen, until
there, atop a rock, sits an elderly gentleman
he smokes a pipe and listens
with euphoric attention to
the blare of a less than modern machine
he hails me in gallant fashion
just as one might expect
I stop aware I have found the past right here
touching today
Stimulus replacing stillness
This, the Rock Garden
Still contemporary, still present

Jane Richardson

The Handkerchief Tree

Chengtu, Szechwan,   7th September 1869

My dear family,
        I have recently been working, like Our Lord himself, as a carpenter! I have built three strong chests to protect my plants and insects, bird skins and mammal skins, on their long journey from here to Shanghai and on to Paris. I am sending this letter with them, praying that all will arrive safely. I will soon make the five-day trek back to the College at Muping, my base since the beginning of March. I hope you will receive the letter I sent in April, reporting my first exciting discovery, of a white bear. I had heard rumours of it, but suspected that it might, like the dragon, be a mythical creature. Since my hunters brought me that first, young one, I have seen a live adult, also with small black ears, black eye patches, black limbs and a black band across the back. The bear feeds on bamboo and is the prettiest mammal I have ever seen.
        Since then, I have spent all my time searching for new species, ascending to at least 4,500 metres, where the air is very thin and I can see, gleaming far away, the Large Snowy Mountains, perhaps the highest in the world. The slopes here are covered in mixed forest, dominated by tall firs and pines, and deciduous species of many kinds which I have never seen before.

The most remarkable tree, which I found at 2,000 metres, looks as though it is covered in white lace handkerchiefs which flutter in the breeze, so that I found myself thinking of Momia, waving to me as I left home on numerous occasions, and felt quite melancholy as I remembered you all. You are daily in my thoughts and prayers. But I digress. The 'handkerchiefs' are not flowers, but bracts, white leaf-like structures which act like petals, attracting pollinators. I hope that the seeds, which I am sending to M. Baillon at the Jardin des Plantes, will germinate. All my specimens here are hard-won, as it was so icy and bitterly cold at first, and so hot and humid in summer. Often there are no paths and I have to force my way through tangles of vine and bramble. There are gorgeously coloured hydrangeas and rhododendrons, and wild fruit trees, in fact the 'handkerchief tree' was beside a large cherry tree and some figs with very sweet fruit. But enough of botany!

Thomé, my trustworthy helper, is well. I have recently been ill with fever again, but am recovering. I am not sure how long I shall stay in the mountains. The Lord bless you and keep you,
Armand

Barbara Mearns

Perpetuity

moving in unison the trees scream
their young branches wrenched
from the parent bough

a summer storm the wind insistent
bullying
overwhelming obliteration

tho destroyed those limbs
will reconnect
reunite as an arboreal family

from birth our lives are finite
sustained by the evergreen
family tree

where each of us will find a place
by those we have loved and
those we never knew

Continuity assured

Jane Richarson

New Beginnings

After many dreich and drizzly days, it is a pleasure to
stroll in the sunshine on the Crichton Grounds.
Uplifting and reviving.
Nature's reminder of Spring's arrival
A special time of year when plants and living creatures
return to life.
Hearing a buzz, I 've spotted a drone in the bushes in
search of a queen,
Above me I can see a goldfinch tweeting joyfully on a
branch.
Happiness is in the air.
Now I find myself thinking of the souls who had been
confined to the Lunatic Asylum within these grounds
many years ago.
Had they been allowed to venture outside into a garden
and feel the sun on their weary brows?
Hopefully some saw new life begin and prayed that they
too might recover and live once more to smell the
flowers.

Eleanor Chesters

Fairy Tale

There is a place I seek
it's not on any map I've seen
I'll set off into the unknown
ask directions on the way.

Birdwatcher on the road instructs me,
Find the tree where the blackcap sings.
The blackcap's flourish transfixes me —
a fluting chatter of repeated notes.

Lady on a bench sits sketching.
I look where she is looking
see an endless expanse of sky
no clouds on the far horizon.

In the field below she shows me,
two hares, ears laid flat
hunkered down and well disguised
as two brown stones.

She says, you don't need directions
walk on till sunset and you'll be there.
Above in the blue blue, two ravens
cronk and frolic, flip over and back.

I arrive home in the nearly dark
my mapless journey surely done
at last realise this thing I sought
has always been within me.

                                    Leonie Ewing

Crichton College: Lasting Learning, Lasting Memories

In 2000 I became one of the second yearly intake of students in Glasgow University's new Crichton Liberal Arts College, housed in the conjoined Rutherford and McCowan buildings. There were nearly sixty other students, a large increase over the numbers in the first intake. I was taking the first steps in a three-year M.A. course, and a journey that in a real way is still continuing.

From the start my experience was very different from the way I remembered my first time at Uni, at the Glasgow campus. The courses were stimulatingly different, and I was different, thirty years later. We were all mature students (two, at least, were 70) who hadn't just experienced life but interrogated it as well. That gave us context in which to set, and absorb, what we were learning. We approached the courses actively; it was a two-way process, bringing out lots of queries and comments from us in tutorials, when we would ask for and get more information from out tutors. We were eager for it and in turn we responded better to the teaching.

We had a good rapport with most of the teaching staff, being level with them in personal maturity at least. They in turn must have enjoyed the fact (as Ted Cowan told us he did) that we weren't just unresponsive 18-year-olds blankly staring in at best semi-comprehension at a pictorial representation of Plato's theory of Forms, for example. On one or two occasions, we must have surprised lecturers visiting from the main campus whom we wouldn't allow to treat us like five-year-olds who, not yet knowing any better, would just passively swallow any fairy-tale in the form of dubious ideology disguised as intellectualism.

I remember the philosophy club, where we decided order was just a special condition of chaos. I really warmed to philosophy (my 18-year-old self would have found that incomprehensible), existentialism in particular.

I met some remarkable people, in particular my Buddhist friend Tina. After her tragic death, I read one of her essays. The mind was still boggling a week later. Others of us, Vivien Jones, Kathy Forbes, and Isobel Gibson went on to be founder-members of Crichton Writers.

Alas, "up the road" the university authorities were becoming unhappy with Crichton's continuance in its current form. At a meeting, at Crichton (!), its fate as a liberal arts college was sealed. The formidable Wendy Downes organised and led a walk from Dumfries to Glasgow to present the case for its survival. In vain.

There were other memories that still sustain me. The wonderful end-of-session parties have even come up in dreams where we all get together again. The nostalgia hasn't faded, even yet.

Ian McQueen

Crichton Campus 2011

My little Honda locked with a light clunk and flash of orange light. I slid the key into the pocket of my chinos and swung my canvas bag over my shoulder. The curving path ahead was scattered with amber-jewelled leaves. High in the canopies of oak, ash and beech raucous jackdaws squabbled. I hugged my fleece around me to thwart crisp morning air and walked towards the red sandstone building ahead, a 1930s block-shape, secure and confident in its parkland estate.

I pushed through heavy doors into a hushed space of knowledge and learning. A corridor door opened ahead and students thronged past with exclamations of 'Wowsers!', 'I freaked!' and 'How do they expect us to....', amid bursts of laughter. I watched the shifting mass of long hair, leggings, sweatshirts and skinny jeans and thought of the hard hours of study to gain a place on an Environmental or Nursing degree with the respective universities on the campus. I was tipping nearer to seventy years than seventeen and hoping to develop skills in creative writing. The open lay-out café offered an orange plastic chair and I settled in to wait for my tutor, David.

He greeted me warmly, 'Coffee?'

'Yes, please, an Americano, just black.'

'Good choice, that's my brew too, let's take our drinks to my room'.

We ascended more flights of stairs than the exterior of the building had led me to expect. David chatted on as we entered a rabbit-warren of rooms at the top under the wing of the School of Interdisciplinary Studies. My tutor reassured me that there were no formal entry requirements for the course due to start in a few weeks. Students would experiment with thematic and stylistic issues such as voice, dialogue, description and setting. I itched to get started, it was just what I needed. We would present pieces we'd written in workshops and hear comments from our peers. The peers from my course would be mainly young students in their second year of a degree and the majority of them would be from overseas. My toes curled as I wondered what today's bright, young intake might make of my scribblings. David completed the requisite paperwork with me and I was on the course.

A breeze sped me along as the heavy doors of Rutherford McCowan building clanked behind me. I was glad to be out in the fresh air, much as I had enjoyed the chat with my tutor. The top wing had rather unsettled me. As I made my way along a winding corridor, I felt a chill rush of air when a door opened to reveal a spiralling wooden staircase. It reminded me of steps to the gallery of a church I knew which were said to be haunted. *What was ghosting the garret here?*

The building had been part of Crichton Royal Institution, a psychiatric hospital which, though forward looking in its time, undertook treatment by leeches and purging and other rituals which made me shudder. Even more ghoulish was the practice of lobotomy in the hope of curing patients before the advent of modern-day drugs. I recalled that the hospital had become known as a ground-breaking facility for treating alcoholism in the 1960s. There had been gossip locally of underground passages for the purpose of moving celebrity patients around the hospital complex, far away from prying eyes. Did they still exist? *Would phantoms inhabit them now?*

I shook my head and sent such spurious thoughts on the wind.

On impulse, my steps took me further through the beautifully kept Crichton estate. I walked past Elizabeth Crichton, resplendent in bronze, serenely overlooking the astounding legacy she had created. Crichton Church was firmly closed and the original Crichton Hall obscured by trees. I soon found myself in the rock garden musing on a bench beside a pool thronged with aquatic plants and water lilies. A blackbird rootled in the undergrowth. My husband had been a patient at the Crichton a few years before due to a nervous breakdown. I saw the first tentative signs of his recovery one day when he noticed, in wonder, the abundant foliage of lofty trees in the grounds. I recalled too a harrowing visit forty years before to a long-term patient in Crichton Royal Hospital as we called it then. Now, the modern mental health facility, Midpark, would open nearby. The last mental health patients were due to be transferred soon and Crichton Royal would be finally closed. Crichton Campus was to be the next chapter.

I resolved to take David's advice and ask to join Crichton Writers, a group which met here on the campus and welcomed anyone with a resolve to develop their writing. A new chapter for me too.

Christine Ashworth

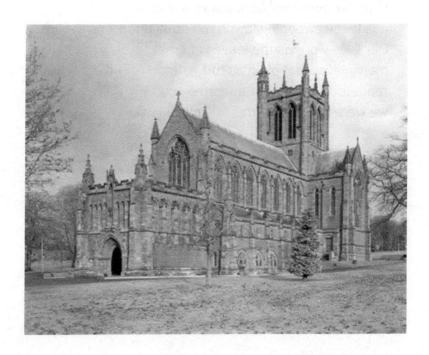

As Leaves of Grass

If you want me again, look for me under your boot soles.
Walt Whitman

All around you here, remembrances —
built into buildings, consecrations,
plaques, cenotaphs, even the humble
benches named. None speak of us.
Our keepers register as monumental,
commended to their greater glory.

Find our memorial beneath your feet —
it is these sweeping lawns you stroll upon.
Our lives were as the leaves of grass,
mown level, laid plain as turf, grief
rendered regular. Innumerable now,
we were made to fit this tidy place.

Our hopes kept short in the long days,
time rolled even in those many seasons
we were left to compost in this bin.
Recall in truth the hard history
of the place — lying deep beneath
that sward, our fevered dreams.

Robin Leiper

THE ASYLUM
AN EFFORT OF EMPATHY

Mad for it

Madness is superior to temperance because the latter has a merely human origin while the former belongs to the divine.   Plato

Before

you set off, up the middle road & round the bend –
go out to lunch but still one sandwich short of a picnic –
become unhinged, unglued – *run amok or berserk* –
lose it – the plot, your mind, your rag –
flip out, freak out, wig out –
crack up, break down, boil over –
come apart at the seams OR
do your nut or be beside yourself –

blow a fuse or gasket, your top or stack, *your mind* –
go crazy, haywire, postal, ape, ballistic or to pieces –
BE loco, psycho, wacko, cuckoo/
bonkers, crackers, nuts / potty, kooky, loopy, loony,
wacky, barmy, batty / and
off your head, the rails, the wall, your rocker or
the deep end

prior to all this...
notice please
it seems you think a lot and speak with such a mixture
of enthusiasms
     of the matter —
might it be you're mad for it?
     this is your crazy-love

Robin Leiper

Crichton Royal Hospital 1971

'Do you remember Jon? My friend who was hurt in a logging accident. It's ... a brain injury, he's paralysed.' My heart plummeted to see my fiancé distraught. 'Thing is, his mum likes him to have visitors. I guess she's hoping against hope for a glimmer of recognition somewhere. Would you come with me to the Crichton to see him?'

Jon's mother, Betty, met us outside Crichton Church. 'Have you been here before? We'll go through the main building first.' She was youthful and chic and I knew that she was intent on making the visit as pleasant as she could. She led us through a large sitting area. Golden light streamed through the windows. A dapper, white-haired gent was tinkling the piano keys and waving from time to time to people on couches around the room. The tune seemed to evaporate towards the moulded ceilings stained with tobacco smoke. A patient sat heavily on a settee in the window area and dust motes snagged in the sun's rays. 'Isn't it lovely that residents can enjoy this bright room?' Betty said. The music stopped and I looked back to see the pianist stand up. Stains of dried excrement spattered his trousers.

We left the sunroom behind and entered a single storey building by a corridor decorated in drab greens and browns. Sparse furnishings were from over thirty years before. In the waiting room a lady nestled in an armchair suddenly gesticulated wildly and made high-pitched, unrecognisable chatter. A nurse came and led her gently away.

Jon was in a hospital bed in a small room. His gaze did not leave us as we strived to talk about anything which might prompt a memory. I was glad that his mum was there to guide our chat but I could see little response from him.

We stepped out into the well-tended grounds where trees soughed and sighed. I took a tight hold of my lad's arm and breathed in deeply, the scent of newly cut grass tickling my nostrils. He pulled me close. 'Thank you for coming with me,' he whispered, 'thank you.'

Christine Ashworth

Mother in Crichton
They say she has lost her mind
My heart is broken

Eleanor Chesters

I'm Coming

amongst buddleia   hydrangea   roses   sweet
peas
Welsh poppies   time heavy on hands   deep in flower
beds
felt the caress of soil   listened
to the sycamore   leaves rippling in the canopy above

talked to squirrels   rabbits   poured secrets into
their ears
but only the wind   knows my real name

now   gardens hunker down
daisies   buttercups   blades of grass   stand vigil
outside this window
lone crow's lament   a scour of the sky
and in the soon-to-be-dark of this not-home
room   bland walls breathe
in   frailty   out   loss

like coloured marbles   scraps of conversation roll
 under the door   no map   for these words

time folds tight   its wings
slackens   fear and pain   living ebbs away
a last breath   the only voice left   takes flight
through the open window
tha mi a'tighinn

I

Kriss Nichol

Always the Turning Earth

Up early, she'd often let things slip.
Distracted, in a half-forgotten dream

she'd give herself away like yesterday
biting her lip as the cup hit the floor

a rhyming scheme she used before
admission, written on the window

whispered its Latin name. But at
other times, like today, birds came

and filled the trees with song; spring
again and always the turning earth

the push and pull of leaf and tide; moons
that wax and wane; suns that rise and rise and rise
again.

Clare Phillips

I was born of storms

I was born of storms.
The wind howled through the cracked windowpane.
Drunken roars from my father, then shattering crash of
dishes against the wall.
Rumble of thunder before the flash of lightning tore the
sky apart.
It will pass, my mother said.
I did not believe her.

The angels started whispering to me at night.
'You are evil, a blot upon the world, a reject of society'.
Sleep became a living nightmare.
It will pass, my mother said.
I did not believe her.

The shadow of a little girl began to lead me.
She took me down dangerous tracks,
across cliff edges, daring me to step closer.
She laughed when I refused to jump.
They put me in the Crichton when the voices got too
loud.
I got some peace there, helping in the gardens.
Still the angels kept me awake at night.

Going to chapel was my sanctuary.
The sunlight streamed through the windows,
made patterns on the marble floor.

Huddled on the bench,
it was then that I saw her,
The Mother of God,
standing in the light with diamonds in her hair.
Her slippers made of solid gold,
glinted like a thousand candles.
Her hands outstretched, she spoke only to me.
I breathed her scent in wonder.
Hail Mary, Saviour of souls,
wash the stains of despondency from my face.
Bring me peace in my hour of despair.

Carol Price

Possibility

The Rock Garden, Crichton Royal Institution

Those endless afternoons
huddled trembling by the pool
or perched half-way upon the sandstone steps.

Vegetation crowded round
all eyes and ears.
Who else would listen?

Sometimes an audience
to mock or sigh and turn away
sometimes to quiver with you.

The trees held quietly apart.
No sympathy — only that glimpse
of possibility: you also might endure.

Robin Leiper

Lady C

'Madam, tea is served in the parlour.'

'I'm just coming, Betsy. I'm trying to get the right colour for this rose. I can't find that nice pink paint.'

'I'll have a look, Madam.'

Betsy has heard this many times and wondered if Lady C was having one of her difficult days. Still, she applied herself to the paints in the tiered box that had been used for many years. Two reds, but not the one she sought apparently. Her employer was becoming a little agitated now and Betsy hoped tea might help. She had baked scones in the morning. Betsy escorted Lady C to the apartment and poured tea. The scones, however, were rejected as the missing paint became a persistent thought.

The next day the sun shone and Dr Browne suggested a session outdoors. The ladies walked the short distance to the Rock Garden. Lady C was in the most affable of mood and established herself near the lily pond. The rose of yesterday seemed forgotten. Instead, she chose a pretty yellow flowering bush, the sun just catching it and enhancing the colour. A pleasant time elapsed until, quite suddenly, Lady C pointed at Mrs. B sitting nearby and shouted,

'You've got my ochre!'

Mrs. B smiled at her and said nothing. A nurse approached Lady C.

'Shall we look in your box?' Whereupon the box was knocked unceremoniously to the ground where it landed in a puddle. Neither the ochre nor the rosy pink was evident. The paints wiped and returned to their box, Lady C once more harangued the unfortunate Mrs. B who continued to paint in serene fashion. Betsy was summoned. Lady C was escorted back to her apartment.

Doctors considered Lady C to be fit for discharge but her family suggested a little longer. In fact, it is true Lady C found the hospital with its beautiful grounds, comfortable accommodation and excellent nourishment a most agreeable location. Lately, however, she had found reason to accuse Mrs. B of all manner of misdemeanour, always associated with their painting. It was an unfortunate setback.

The following weekend both ladies were present at one of the regular theatre productions in the hospital. The residents took great pleasure in these events and Lady C was in good humour. She was in such good humour that she was polite and friendly towards Mrs. B. They watched the presentation and took tea together afterwards. As Mrs. B rose from her chair she had the misfortune to trip on a fold in the carpet. Nurses came at once to her aid, and as they helped her upright a cascade of paint brushes and paints fell from beneath her voluminous gown. At once Lady C was on her hands and knees.

'I knew it! There they are. *My* pink and ochre. And that brush is mine too!'

At this several other people crowded round the fallen objects, exclaiming at their lost belongings. Dignity departed as they joined Lady C on the floor.

Mrs. B, however, was quite unconcerned. As she watched the nurses collect myriad brushes and paints, she gently remonstrated that *her* work required them all.

Jane Richardson

Sky Lit

"for the furious, fatuous and lunatic poor"

You might glimpse her spectre
on some snell December morning,
ghosting a frosted windowpane,
wan in the thin light of the waste
within those pallid, shrunken decades

Outwith what seems, she sky-lights
across the long and weary days,
fades out of focus and away and
speculates, through grey shades
and the blue, toward the far beyond

Drifts amidst her cloud of dreams
listening for the lilt of angels,
slips through hairline cracks between
the worlds, soars clear of bonds that
chain the rest to heart-sob earth

She found herself inside a briar palace,
the spell or curse of somebody's idea
of safety, left to the care of thorns
and hope, that she alone might
sculpt from it her own deliverance

And so she sometimes did

Robin Leiper

Take it off the wall and hide it in the cupboard

There, on the Museum wall
hang the works of lunatics and sots.
Private innermost thoughts and screams,
and everything else in between.
Manifested on paper, card and board,
some on canvas rendered in oils.
Slashes of bright colour faded by time,
pastels floating dreams on to paper.
Landscapes, portraits and abstracts,
subtracted from the depths of psyche,
troubled and misunderstood.
Images from the wealthy and famous,
And from the poor and invisible.
All suffering from afflictions,
that no one really understood.

                              Christine Cameron

Mirror Image

Saw himself by chance -
mirror showed a rotting
skull, maggots writhed
where eyes once smiled.

He ran wildly, arms waving,
screams made his throat
raw, they caught him -
they asked what happened.

When they heard their disbelief
almost convinced him,
they tried to show him -
fear unseated his reason.

Idée Fixe

On a wheel, semblance of spinning,
threads twist endlessly around,
seem to have no sense like
chance caught dream thoughts
held unwanted in a mind
that long ago was frozen
into one repeated moment
flickering through time.

Struggle

Grey days passed in uniformity,
they took her into the garden
showed her sunlit beauty
she could not reach it.

Tears like raindrops ran down
her lovely face, her weary smile
did not light her eyes, she knew
their care for her was undeserved.

She was dutiful, made no trouble,
hid behind a bright smile, appeared
'normal', they became less watchful
eventually discharged her.

Her inner struggle lasted years,
finally she saw no reason to go on,
longed for peace – she took a walk –
they found her in the drifted snow.

Anne Micklethwaite

The only way out is through...
after Blue Landscape by Archie Sutter Watt

Step over and out
of it – that same page,
the next stage – and
start to feel the free
of falling.

Hit the churn and dark
rock rapids, find
your black and blue.
Grin and bear
the din and glare
of plunging

into iced indigo
chill cerulean
and burst
on the dawn
hosed out
over a green world

drifting above your
complementary yellows
with the dangerous
expectation of
a soft landing

Robin Leiper

68

THE PRESENT
AN ANIVERSARY REFLECTION

The Statue of Elizabeth Crichton Speaks

Here I sit, cast in bronze by sculptor Bill Scott and unveiled by HRH The Prince Charles, Duke of Rothesay, on 19th May 2000. I cradle, in my left hand, a small portrait of my dear James, as I gaze out over the Estate we founded nearly two hundred years ago. What a beautiful, peaceful place this is, with the original gardens, rockery and arboretum Dr. Browne and I created, still cared for and now open to the people of Dumfries to enjoy. To my left is the Easterbrook building with its large concert hall, bistro, spa and refurbished swimming pool. To my right is the magnificent Crichton Memorial Church, completed in 1897 in memory of James and me. Behind me is Johnstone House, previously the Laundry, now the Holiday Inn, providing accommodation for visitors. Although I cannot see my original William Burns' Crichton Hall, I know this precious building, so close to my heart, is still there. Now it is no longer needed as a hospital for mental patients, I hear that it has been sold to become a five-star hotel, but that work has yet to begin. Dumfries needs a large, elegant and prestigious hotel and I sincerely hope and pray that this development will take place soon, as I hear whispers that this building is in a very dilapidated condition.

However, my greatest joy and delight is that my original dream has, at last, been realised and the Crichton Estate of 85 acres is now a well-respected

College and University Campus and thriving innovative Business Park, managed by the Crichton Trust. It is now part of the University of Glasgow, the University of the West of Scotland, Dumfries and Galloway College and houses Scotland's Open University, Bell Nursing College, the Carbon Trust and the farm has now become Scotland's Rural University College. This is infinitely more than James and I ever envisaged and gives me great pleasure and satisfaction. Recently, a grant of £975,710 has been awarded to the Crichton Trust to create a 21st Century Village with accessible and carbon neutral housing, a Centre for Memory and Wellbeing for Arts Research and Learning and to house the Crichton Royal Archive.

That these projects keep the Crichton Estate connected to medicine, to the land, to learning and to innovation for the benefit of the people of Dumfries, the wider community, and the world, fills me with delight and hope as well as humility and pride, in equal measure. That our efforts should have been so well rewarded and long-lasting, seems little more than a miracle. Our dream has indeed, at last, come true.

Beverley Vaux

Crichton

inspiration

a scene of great beauty

to paint to write to learn to play

to comprehend those labelled lunatic

ease minds in trouble and confused

a model example

of how to heal

Crichton

Jane Richardson

"Analysis of Significance"

on Appendix 7-3 of the Crichton Campus,
Ladyfield Hall Heritage Appraisal

Of course, there's always that —

the quest for meaning

hermeneutic moment

analysis of significance.

You look at it. And ponder.

You might think: *Scottish Greek Revival*

You might think: *Slave Money*

You might think: *World of Pain*

You might think: *Development Opportunity*

You might go on...

It all depends on who you are.

You might think: *Who am I?*

Robin Leiper

75

NOTES

Historical Material: The letter, journal entry and short story are, of course, each re-imagined by the authors but are based on the available historical evidence; in particular, they draw upon Morag Williams, *History of Crichton Royal Hospital 1839-1989* (DGH1/6/18/209) and on google entries for Elizabeth and James Crichton.

The Handkerchief Tree: There are two Handkerchief Trees in the Crichton Gardens. This rare and distinctive species is named *Davidia involucrata* after Père Armand David, the first Westerner to find one. Père David, a Basque, was a Lazarist priest, famous for his arduous travels in China from 1862-74. During his second expedition, to Sichuan, he collected 145 mammal species, 441 bird species and 676 kinds of plants, which he sent back to France. This letter is fictional but based on his diaries. B.M.

The Horticultural Show: I came across a flyer for a horticultural show at the Crichton while browsing the wonderful on-line collection held by the Welcome Collection. Many of the records are not yet digitized but there are two scrapbooks available which contain a wealth of information. This horticultural show is not dated but presumed to have occurred in the late 1800's. You can find the flyer in Recreation and Printing Scrapbook. 1842-1947 (DGH1/6/17/2) C.P.

Perpetuity: This poem came from a comment made by the late Bill Wigram after a storm up at the Crichton which destroyed so many trees. In his sage fashion, which we so miss, he just said `Looks horrific — but they will grow again'. J.R.

I'm Coming: tha mi a'tighinn is the title in Scots Gaelic.

Lady C: Lady C is imagined. I thought she might have lived in the top tier of hospital accommodation, as recorded in the archives. Some patients were able to bring their own attendants which is why Betsy is there. Mrs. B, however, is based on a painter of some renown, also a patient. The behaviour of the artist, Joanna Hutton, is described in *Art in Madness* by Maureen Park 2010. Mrs. Hutton arrived at the Crichton in 1847 and died there in 1856. J.R.

Mirror Image: A serious mental condition involving a breakdown in the relation between thought, emotion and behavior leading to faulty perception, inappropriate actions and feelings, withdrawal from reality and personal relationships into fantasy and delusion, and a sense of mental fragmentation. A.M.

Idee Fixe: An idea or desire that dominates the mind, an obsession. A.M.

Struggle: Depression is a common but serious mood disorder. It causes severe symptoms that affect how a person feels, thinks and handles daily activities, such as sleeping, eating or working.

Illustration Credits

Dr Flora Murray (Bank of Scotland £100 note, detail) p18: Christine Ashworth

Handkerchief Tree p39: Christine Dudgeon

Spring Blossom, Crichton p41:- Bob Leiper

Statue of Elizabeth Crichton p65: Eleanor Chesters

The remaining images are used by kind permission of NHS Dumfries and Galloway Crichton Royal Hospital Collection, held by the Heritage Service, Dumfries and Galloway Council: -

Dr James Crichton of Friars Carse (by J.G.McL.Arnott) & Mrs Elizabeth Crichton (unknown artist) p6; Crichton Institution 19th century p12; Dr W.A.F. Browne p15; Crichton from the North East p41 (unknown artist); All other images are paintings by anonymous inmates of the Asylum and part of the collection of their art started by Dr Browne.

Author Biographies

Christine Ashworth has been a member of CWs for 13 years. She is inspired by the natural world and the changes in man's connection with it over the years. Christine likes to write short stories.

Christine Cameron is originally a Londoner. She has a degree in art and design and worked in design and publishing. As a mature student, she gained an MA Hons. in Liberal Arts with Environmental Studies and an MSc. in Carbon Management at the Crichton Campus of Glasgow University. She lives in Nithsdale, an inspirational location for all environmental and creative diversions.

Eleanor Chesters found in her job as a Primary Teacher, that she was constantly creating ideas from themes, so children could express themselves and perform. She especially enjoyed this part of the work and it seemed natural after retirement to join Crichton Writers.

Leonie Ewing is a retired biologist and farmer with a lifelong interest in science and natural history, now enjoying writing both poetry and prose in Wigtownshire. She enjoys the challenge of showing that arts and science share the creative process. She is a past chair of Crichton Writers.

Robin Leiper is a psychologist and psychotherapist. His poetry has been published in various magazines and anthologies. He won the Seahorse pamphlet competition in 2022 and the Wigtown Festival Fresh Voice award of 2023.

Ian McQueen Is the eternal student, sorry scholar, He can boast several long incomplete pieces of writing and three Gaelic poems published plus a self-published short biography of a deceased friend.

Barbara Mearns' writing experience includes 20 years as editor for *A Rocha International*, scientific papers and short notes on wildlife; press releases and published poetry.

Together with her husband she has written books on the early naturalists (see www.mearnsbooks.com).

Anne Micklethwaite joined Crichton Writers shortly after she moved to Scotland. Her work has appeared for a number of Crichton Writers' anthologies, and in *Southlight* magazine. In 2022 she published *A Cup of Tea and a Poem,* a slim volume of her poetry.

Kriss Nichol's poetry and short stories have appeared in numerous small press magazines and anthologies. She has been both highly commended and a prize winner in competitions, has published three poetry pamphlets, a sequence of haibun, and two novels.

Linda Powell has loved the English language since she was tiny and always enjoyed writing. Membership of two local writing groups has been a joy for her and her small output, mostly poetry now, has been published in group anthologies.

Clare Phillips, following success in local competitions, will launch her first full collection *Here to Stay* in August 2024. Published by Drunk Muse Press, it brings together poems from her early life with those inspired by living and working in Scotland, including time spent training professionals on the Crichton Campus.

Carol Price is a Dubliner living in the Scottish borders. Since retirement, writing has become an addictive, time-eating occupation. She runs a creative writing group in Annan called The Writeyard and writes poetry, short stories, with several incomplete novels dragging her into fictional dilemmas.

Jane Richardson joined Crichton Writers in 2013, just in time for the 10th Anniversary. The enjoyment of meeting like minds, writing together, and learning so much, has been a joy. She writes both prose and poetry, has contributed to the anthologies and to other publications.

Scott Thow works as a nurse practitioner in D&G Royal Infirmary. When not doing the night shift, his passion is writing fiction, both short stories and novels.

Beverley Vaux was born in Kent and brought up in Rio de Janeiro. At school alone in England, reading and writing were her vital companions. Life got in the way of writing – secretarial college, working at Buckingham Palace, children and much else. She is thrilled to be in Crichton Writers, finding the Muse again!

Crichton Writers is a collective of writers from across south-west Scotland, originally based at the Glasgow University Crichton Campus in Dumfries.

First formed in 2003 out of a creative writing course led by Tom Pow, the group has gone through many changes over the years but continues to meet monthly for creative workshops, mutual support and critique. It continues to publish anthologies of its members' poems, prose, plays and film writing. It stages readings and performances across southern Scotland and Cumbria.

The Crichton: An Anniversary Re-Imagining is the twentieth anniversary publication of the group.

Previous Publications from Crichton Writers

Wind Fall 2007: writings about gardens and gardening

Scratching the Surface 2008: explorations of the archaeology of Dumfries & Galloway

Words & Bronze 2009: responses to the work of sculptor Elizabeth Waugh (DVD and performance)

I Remember, I Remember 2010 memoir in poetry & prose

A Banquet of Writing 2011: food, glorious food enjoyed on the page as well as the plate

Space, Time and Nine Planets 2012: voyages into science through written word performance

10th Anniversary Anthology 2013; an open theme, celebrating the breadth and wealth of members writing

Across the Fence 2015: writing about neighbours and neighbourliness

Alchemy 2017: Annandale and the New Distillery publication and performance (mentioned in the Scottish Parliament)

Trees 2018: postcard poems and images

No Stone Unturned 2021: linked to the Dumfries Stone Carving Project in conjunction with Dumfries Museum, publication and several performances

Through The Lens 2022: responses to photographs and how we frame what is seen

BV - #0019 - 100624 - C11 - 210/148/5 - PB - 9781838299705 - Matt Lamination